Wilma Wilderness's

Guide to...

BUGS

Written by
Charis Mather

KidHaven
PUBLISHING

Published in 2026 by
KidHaven Publishing, an Imprint of Greenhaven Publishing, LLC
2544 Clinton St., Buffalo, NY 14224

Written by: Charis Mather
Edited by: Rebecca Phillips-Bartlett
Designed by: Amelia Harris

All facts, statistics, web addresses, and URLs in this book were verified as valid and accurate at time of writing. No responsibility for any changes to external websites or references can be accepted by either the author or publisher.

Cataloging-in-Publication Data
Names: Mather, Charis, 1999-.
Title: Bugs / Charis Mather.
Description: Buffalo, NY : KidHaven Publishing, 2026. | Series: Wilma Wilderness's guide to… | Includes glossary and index.
Identifiers: ISBN 9781534551527 (pbk.) | ISBN 9781534551534 (library bound) | ISBN 9781534551541 (ebook)
Subjects: LCSH: Insects--Juvenile literature.
Classification: LCC QL467.2 M384 2026 | DDC 595.7--dc23

Printed in China

CPSIA compliance information: Batch #QW26KH: For further information contact Greenhaven Publishing LLC at 1-844-317-7404.

All images are courtesy of Shutterstock.com, unless otherwise stated.
Cover – Lauritta, Sandra Standbridge, irin-k, Aleksandar Dickov, isarescheewin. Recurring – AlinArt, haru_natsu_kobo, Kobee, Macrovector. 2–3 – Riko fajar. 4–5 – Marawan A3, corlaffra. 6–7 – TWINS DESIGN STUDIO, Stefan Rotter, OMG_Studio. 8–9 – Nursin Ercetin, mehmetkrc. 10–11 – Achmad Yuge, Mathisa, I Wayan Sumatika, Robert Sanjeev Ross. 12–13 – Cherry Art Pics, Haletska Olha, Mathisa. 14–15 – Jovahn Fischer, sarin nana. 16–17 – Boris Edelmann, Ian Fletcher. 18–19 – Simol1407, Cat_arch_angel, JorgeOrtiz_1976. 20–21 – KRIACHKO OLEKSII, Brian Woolman. 22–23 – Brian A Jackson, TimeImage Production.

Contents

Words that look like this can be found in the glossary on page 24.

A Wilderness of Wonders

Welcome to Wilma Wilderness's Guide to Bugs. My name is Wilma. Bugs are some of my favorite creatures to look for in the wild. Some people think these creepy-crawlies are creepy. Not me!

A minibeast is a small creature with no backbone.

You will find bugs wherever you go—insects, spiders, slugs, worms, and more. This guide will teach you about many types of bugs. The more you know, the better your outdoor explorations will be.

Why We Need Bugs

Many parts of nature depend on bugs. Bugs are food for lots of animals. They help keep the soil healthy by breaking down waste. They pollinate flowers.

When it comes to identifying bugs in the wild, it helps to know a few facts about how they look and behave. Just be warned—not all of these amazing creatures are safe to touch.

Watch out! These fire ants have a painful sting.

Many Kinds of Bugs

There are over a million different kinds of bugs in the wilderness. To help you figure out what kind of bug a creature is, pay attention to its features.

Feature Focus

These questions can help you identify a bug:

All Sorts of Appearances

Insects are a type of bugs with wings and six legs.

Centipedes have long, **segmented** bodies with lot of legs. The segments are protected by a hard covering called an exoskeleton.

Many bugs look very different when they are young. Caterpillars build cocoons to keep themselves safe while their bodies grow wings and become moths or butterflies. This change is called metamorphosis.

Where Bugs Live and What They Eat

Many bugs have mini homes. These are called microhabitats. A microhabitat is a small area that has the specific things a creature needs to survive, such as food and a safe hiding spot.

Dark, damp places make excellent microhabitat homes for many bugs.

Feature Focus

Ask these questions about the environment a bug is in:

Is it dark or light?

Is it damp or dry?

What does the bug need to survive?

What kind of food can be found here?

All Sorts of Habitats

Barnacles live on rocks near the ocean. When the water rises, they open their shells and reach out to find food. When the water lowers, they close their shells so they do not dry out.

Flies have mouthparts that are like spongy straws. They need food they can slurp up. Rotting food and other kinds of waste are often wet and sludgy. This is perfect for flies.

Flies soften food by spitting on it.

Behavior

When watching bugs in the wild, pay attention to their behavior. These little creatures get up to lots of different activities. Each bug is suited to a different kind of work.

Feature Focus

These questions can help you identify a bug:

All Sorts of Behavior

Honey bees work hard to look after their hive and their queen bee. Many honey bees use flower pollen to make honey and wax. They can guide other bees to the flowers by doing a special dance.

Woodlice can often be found in dark places looking for rotten plants and other waste to eat. If needed, some kinds of woodlice can protect themselves by rolling their hard, segmented exoskeletons into a ball.

Wonderfully Wild Bugs

Bugs might be mini, but they can also be mighty. When looking for a mate, male stag beetles use their impressive mouthparts to wrestle other males. These mouthparts are called mandibles.

Some bugs are masters of hiding. Stick insects hide from predators by looking like part of the environment. They can look just like brown or green twigs.

Get Exploring!

Being outdoors is much more interesting when you know about bugs. There are so many to learn about. Next time you are out in the wilderness, keep an eye out for these tiny creatures.

Safety Warning!!!

Remember not to touch bugs in the wild—just look.

Why not start writing your own guide to bugs near you? Write down where you find them, what they look like, and what they are doing. You could even try drawing them!

Glossary

antenne a pair of long, thin sensors found on insects' heads

behave to act in a certain way

cocoons cases that protect caterpillars or larvae as they grow into moths or butterflies

environment the natural world, or something's natural surroundings

hive a structure where bees live; these can be human-made or natural

identifying finding out what something is based on what someone knows about it

mate a partner of the same species that an animal produces young with

pollinate to pass on pollen from one plant to another plant of the same kind so that seeds will be produced

predators animals that hunt other animals for food

segmented made up of similar-shaped sections

Index